JIMMIE RODGERS

Country Music Library

JIMMIE RODGERS

ROBERT K. KRISHEF

Lerner Publications Company ▪ Minneapolis

ACKNOWLEDGMENTS: The illustrations are reproduced through the courtesy of: pp. 6, 12, Country Music Foundation Library and Media Center; pp. 9, 14, 16 (top and bottom), 18, 20, 24, 25, 28, 36, 40, 44, 52, 55, 58, 60, Jimmie Rodgers Memorial Foundation; p. 10, Charles "Fuzzy" Owen; p. 11 (left), RCA; p. 11 (right), Heuck; pp. 33, 48, John Edwards Memorial Foundation; p. 62, Board of Directors of the Country Music Association, Inc.

LIBRARY OF CONGRESS CATALOGING IN PUBLICATION DATA

Krishef, Robert K.
    Jimmie Rodgers.

    (A Country Music Book)
    Discography: p. 63
    Includes index.
    SUMMARY: A biography of country music's first solo recording star, in whose brief career cut tragically short by death he recorded 111 songs that sold twenty million records.

    1. Rodgers, James Charles, 1897-1933 — Juvenile literature. 2. Country musicians — United States — Biography — Juvenile literature. [1. Rodgers, James Charles, 1897-1933. 2. Musicians. 3. Country music] I. Title.

ML3930.R62K7   784'.092'4   [B] [92]   77-90156
ISBN 0-8225-1404-4

Manufactured in the United States of America. Published simultaneously in Canada by J. M. Dent & Sons (Canada) Ltd., Don Mills, Ontario.

International Standard Book Number: 0-8225-1404-4
Library of Congress Catalog Card Number: 77-90156

2   3   4   5   6   7   8   9   10   85   84   83   82   81   80

Contents

Dr. Humphrey Bate and his Possum Hunters were popular country musicians during the 1920s. Their radio performances helped to make country music widely known and to pave the way for the career of Jimmie Rodgers.

The Father of Country Music

Country music was born in the small, isolated rural communities of the southern and south-eastern United States. There, hardship and daily struggles for survival were a basic part of life. The people in the rural South farmed for a living, dug for coal, cut timber, kept stores, and worked on the railroads. Their enemies were the rocky soil, mine cave-ins, foul weather, and sometimes sheer physical exhaustion. And their only relief during hard times was music.

Music has always been an important means of self-expression for hard-working Americans, and it was especially so for generations of people from the South. Through music, they could laugh and cry. Some of their songs helped them forget about their troubles, while other songs helped them work out their problems. But no matter what kind of songs people sang, they felt better because of their music.

For many years, the music of the rural South had no name. It was just music, the same kind of music that had helped generations of working folk through good times and bad. But about 50 or 60 years ago, this special music did get a name—"hillbilly." Later, hillbilly music became known as country and western music, or just plain country music.

People from the city did not really understand this hillbilly sound and often joked about it. Other folks simply ignored it. But attitudes began to change as radio became more popular in the 1920s. Country music programs were among the most popular of the first radio shows, and country music records sold by the millions. Slowly, record companies and radio stations began to realize the commercial possibilities of such music.

Today everyone recognizes the importance of country music. That does not mean that everybody likes this kind of music, anymore than everyone likes rock or classical music. But when Americans spend an estimated $400 million annually on country records and tapes, there can be no doubt that country music has become a big business.

Although no one person was responsible for the current popularity of country music, there was somebody who "got the ball rolling." His name was Jimmie Rodgers. This physically frail but spirited singer was country music's first solo recording star in the late 20s and early 30s. His career lasted only

Jimmie Rodgers, the Singing Brakeman

six years, but in that short time, he recorded 111 songs and sold an estimated 20 million records—second only to Enrico Caruso, the great opera singer of that period.

Jimmie Rodgers, known to millions as the "Singing Brakeman" because he had worked on the railroad, died in 1933. He was only 35 at the time and at the height of his popularity. His records were eagerly bought by millions of Americans—people who hardly had enough money for food. During the Depression, 75 cents was a lot of money for a record, and country folks had to hoard their pennies for months for the special purchase. But then the time would come when they could afford the latest Jimmie Rodgers record at the general store, along with the usual dozen eggs.

*Jimmie Rodgers influenced
many young singers, including
Merle Haggard* (left), *Elvis
Presley,* and *Johnny Cash* (op-
posite page, left and right).

Since the 1930s, Rodgers has been a model for other professional entertainers. For 30 years Hank Snow has been singing railroad songs in the tradition of the "Singing Brakeman." The yodels of Gene Autry and others were patterned after those of Rodgers. And the era of the western cowboy singer began, in part, because of Rodgers, who adopted Texas as his native state. Veteran singing star Ernest Tubb feels that three quarters of modern country singers have been influenced by the style and techniques of Jimmie Rodgers.

Many of today's leading stars had not yet been born or were only youngsters when Rodgers died. But they all grew up listening to his records and learning his style, which combined the characteristics of pop, folk, hillbilly, jazz, and blues. Such diverse singers as Johnny Cash, Merle Haggard, and Elvis Presley have said that they learned from Jimmie Rodgers and that he paved the way for them. Rodgers' influence is felt even among the youngest country western stars—Johnny Rodriguez, for example, developed his style by listening to the songs of Rodgers and Haggard.

Of course, Rodgers himself learned from the people who preceded him. There were several country singers, including Vernon Dalhart, Fiddlin' John Carson, Wendell Hall, and Carson Robison, who made records before Rodgers did. Nor was Rodgers the first yodeler to be recorded. Riley Puckett, for one, had been yodeling on records a full three years before Rodgers. Goebel Reeves, an old-time performer known as the

"Texas Drifter," claimed that he was the one who taught Jimmie how to yodel.

No performer, however, could touch the heart as Jimmie Rodgers did. His yodels had a thrilling, wailing rhythm that made them unique. And the yodels that he used in blues rose from his soul with such great feeling that he came to be known as the "Blue Yodeler." Even though Rodgers had learned to yodel from other singers, he was the one to make the sound a part of country music.

Whether singing, yodeling, or playing his guitar, Rodgers was an entertainer with whom listeners could identify. He was one of them; he spoke their language. Like many listeners, he was a rural southerner who understood the feeling of poverty. He was a family man who had experienced sorrow, and he had been a railroad worker who knew loneliness. Worst of all, poor health bothered Jimmie throughout his life—"My time ain't long," he had said shortly before his death. Although Jimmie's blues songs were heartfelt, he was basically an optimist. He was a cheerful man who always faced the future with courage.

Jimmie Rodgers' reputation has grown along with that of country music. When Jimmie died, country music was far from being the big industry that it is today. The term "country music" hadn't even been invented yet. But now that country music is an important part of the entertainment industry, Jimmie's contributions to its growth are clear. As record executive Stephen Sholes said, Rodgers "directly caused the sale of more phonographs and guitars and inspired more youngsters to take up singing than any single person before or since." More than any other performer, Jimmie deserves the title "Father of Country Music."

Jimmie Rodgers at the age of six

Growing Up 2

James Charles Rodgers was born September 8, 1897, in Meridian, Mississippi. His father, Aaron Rodgers, was a section foreman on the Mobile and Ohio railroad. Aaron Rodgers, like other fathers of that time, probably thought that his son would follow in his footsteps. And why shouldn't he? The 1890s, after all, was the decade of the railroad. Powerful steam locomotives, or "iron horses," had become the new champions of transportation, symbols of progress in conquering distance. The railroad tied one end of the land to the other.

Railroads and the people who worked on them soon became the subjects of songs and stories. John Henry, for example, was a black railroad construction worker who had become a legend by the early 1870s. Known for his feats of strength, John Henry used two 20-pound hammers, one in each hand, to beat the then-new steam drill in a rock-drilling contest. And in 1900, three years after

Left: *Eliza Bozeman Rodgers, Jimmie's mother*
Below: *Jimmie's birthplace in Meridian, Mississippi*

Jimmie Rodgers was born, the famous train engineer Casey Jones took his tragic last ride, which also became a legend. With his hand on the brake, Jones rode to a fiery death in a collision with another train. Casey Jones' trip to the "promised land" was soon immortalized in ballads that were to become a part of Jimmie's boyhood.

Railroading was all Jimmie ever knew as a boy. His mother had died when he was only four, leaving him with a father who moved from place to place in search of work. Young Jimmie had little chance at a normal home life, because Aaron Rodgers took him everywhere he went. The twosome lived in a series of boarding houses and freight yard shanties near Aaron Rodgers' jobs. Jimmie's playgrounds were often nothing more than railroad yards or the cabs of huge locomotives. And his friends were the engineers and the brakemen on the trains. When Jimmie and his dad were on their way from one town to another, the engineers would let Jimmie sit in the cab and pull the whistle cord at road crossings. His childhood was filled with many such experiences.

The people who influenced young Jimmie the most during this time were the blacks who worked on the railroad construction gangs. They let him sit with them while they sang their traditional songs. It was during these sessions that Jimmie listened to the sound of the blues, the crooning,

The train station in Meridian, Mississippi, Jimmie Rodgers' hometown

sometimes painful sound that could stretch one syllable into four. In later years, Jimmie would make use of this informal training in developing his own style—a sort of white man's blues.

Somewhere along the way, Jimmie learned to play the guitar and banjo. For the first time, something other than railroading held his attention. The fascination of music grew so strong for Jimmie that he even began to think about becoming a wandering musician. As Jimmie grew into his teens, he became interested in the show people he saw moving about the country with their tents and carnivals. Such a life of wandering was not new to a boy who had grown up without roots. And as

Jimmie himself traveled from place to place with his father, he found that he had the gift for entertaining others. He even won an amateur talent contest in Meridian, his hometown, where he sang "Bill Bailey" and "Steamboat Bill." By that time, he could accompany himself on the banjo.

Still, nobody doubted that young Jimmie would eventually work on the railroad—that was the only life he knew. His schooling had been so spotty that he had almost no formal education and no special training for a job. Instead he had received a practical education from being around the railroad yard all the time. It was this knowledge that Jimmie used in later years when he wrote songs and made records.

At the age of 14, Jimmie stopped going to school altogether to become a full-time apprentice railroad employee. It was the beginning of a career that would eventually ruin his health and force him into a second career—that of singing.

Working for the Railroad   3

Although Jimmie was only a teenager, his dream of working on the railroad had come true. The first job he was offered was that of assistant foreman — for his father. The title, however, was far more impressive than the duties, which consisted of carrying water to construction crews.

Jimmie was a smart young man. He got along well with other people, and he had drive and determination. As a result of his hard work, he soon got the job of flagman, and then baggage-master. Jimmie's primary goal, however, was to become a regular member of a train crew. In 1914, he was hired by the New Orleans and Northeastern Railroad, which ran between New Orleans, Louisiana, and Meridian, Mississippi. Jimmie was the brakeman, a person who oversaw all the rail cars, coupled and uncoupled them at stops, and performed many other duties.

One of Jimmie's other duties was to throw hobos off the train, a job he found especially hard. Hobos were poor folks, down on their luck, who tried to get free rides by hiding on the boxcars of slow-moving trains. The hobos who hopped a ride on Jimmie's train were lucky, though. Jimmie seldom threw them off, and he often gave them 50 cents for a meal.

For the next 10 years, Jimmie worked as a brakeman on the New Orleans-Meridian run and on other runs in the South. Most of the time, he was happy and satisfied with his work and with his life. He enjoyed reasonably good health at that time, and he had enough money. Jimmie seldom had extra cash, though, for he always spent what he earned. Thriftiness was never one of his strong points.

During this time, Jimmie made the most of his independence and his freedom to travel. Like his father, Jimmie was a restless spirit, always wondering what lay "beyond the next bend." Part of the adventure in Jimmie's life lay in music. As Jimmie traveled around the South, he spent more and more time practicing the guitar and entertaining his friends. He probably didn't realize then how important these hours of practice would be later in life.

Jimmie's guitar and banjo were his constant companions. On long runs, he would reach for one of his instruments and entertain the train crew. A high spot for the crew between journeys was one of Jimmie's informal shows in the caboose or in the roundhouse. Whether a handful of train workers attended or an entire crowd, the applause was always warm. Later in the day, Jimmie would sit by the fire with the black construction workers and sing the blues into the night with them. All these informal concerts inspired him to make even more music.

Jimmie frequently took his guitar or banjo to town, where he played in rowdy bars for money or serenaded young ladies on their front porches. On one of his trips into Meridian, Jimmie met a girl to whom he took a special liking. She was Carrie Williamson, the daughter of a minister. The two young people made a strange pair—Carrie from a conservative family, Jimmie from "the other side of the tracks." Yet Carrie's parents liked Jimmie, and his music added to his natural grace and charm in their eyes. A story has it that Jimmie once serenaded Carrie's ill mother from the street outside her sickroom. Nobody knows whether that story is true, but young Jimmie did win the approval of Carrie's parents. The young couple were married April 7, 1920.

The early years of marriage were a time of great happiness for Jimmie and Carrie. But there were also moments of darkness. Jimmie's health began to fail, and he started missing work. The smoke, soot, and dust of railroading weakened his lungs.

Jimmie Rodgers as a young man

Carrie Williamson Rodgers, Jimmie's bride

And the constant exposure to damp, chilly weather pulled the strength from Jimmie's body faster than he could get well. He caught colds easily and got hacking coughs that he could not shake.

Jimmie missed so much work that he soon lost his job. His illness could not have happened at a worse time, for the railroad boom had come to an end. It was 1918, just after World War I, and jobs were hard to get, especially for a sickly brakeman. Jimmie and Carrie soon learned to do without.

By the early 20s, Jimmie and Carrie had two daughters. Carrie Anita was born in 1921 and June Rebecca in 1923. In December 1923, unhappiness came to the Rodgers family once more—little June died. Jimmie was in New Orleans at the time, looking for work. He had to pawn his banjo to get money enough to come home for his daughter's funeral.

After the funeral, Jimmie became restless and even more upset. He left home once again and soon found steady work with railroads in Colorado and Utah. For the first time in months, he and Carrie had enough money to live decently. But work was not the blessing that it seemed, for the winter was rugged out west. Weather again proved too much for Jimmie Rodgers' frail body.

Poor health forced Jimmie back to Meridian in the spring of 1924. He was pale, ill, and coughing at the time, but in spite of the many symptoms, Jimmie told Carrie not to worry. When he began coughing up specks of blood, the diagnosis was clear. Jimmie had tuberculosis, a very serious disease at the time. In the fall, Jimmie suffered a hemorrhage, a heavy discharge of blood from his damaged lungs. Since the family savings were gone, he was taken to a charity hospital. The doctors thought that Jimmie Rodgers was going to die, but his will to live pulled him through.

Three months after his brush with death, Jimmie left the hospital. The doctors' instructions rang in his ears: "Take care of your health, and give up railroading." Jimmie laughed grimly at the advice. How could he give up railroading? It was all he knew. Yet Jimmie realized that he had to find an answer. His railroading days were over.

A New Career   4

By nature Jimmie Rodgers was a cheerful man, even when he was ill or when jobs were hard to find. During hard times, Jimmie would always say to his wife, "Chin, chin, Mother," meaning "Keep your chin up" or "Don't get discouraged." Carrie often needed encouragement, for she was not as much of an optimist as her husband. Unfortunately, she had plenty of cause for worry in the mid-1920s.

Those were the days when the Rodgers were often moneyless, foodless, and homeless. To keep the family from starving, Carrie Rodgers got jobs as a waitress, a stenographer, and a newsstand clerk. Jimmie, meanwhile, was trying to find steady work but had little luck. Railroading was all that he knew, but he was frustrated with that for many reasons—the most important being his health. For a long time, Jimmie had toyed with the idea of becoming an entertainer, but now he began thinking of it seriously. The question was, could he make a living at performing? Rodgers thought it over and decided that there was no other choice but to try.

For nearly three years, Jimmie searched for a way to get into show business. A common way for a performer to get started at that time was to become a "blackface." In a blackface show, whites would darken their faces with grease or charcoal and sing Negro spirituals and folksongs. Since Jimmie could sing, he decided to become a blackface and join a medicine show. He toured with the show throughout Kentucky and Tennessee, and when times were especially tough he would play and sing on street corners. The nickels and dimes he collected often came from people who were as poor as he.

Working in a medicine show soon became tiresome for Jimmie, so he began to look for new work. He finally joined a dance combo, with his sister-in-law, Elsie McWilliams, on the piano and Slim Rozell on the violin. The three played popular music and waltzes at parties around Meridian, but they did not get many other jobs. Although the combo was not very successful, Jimmie did get to know many different kinds of music. Jimmie also got to know his sister-in-law, who was a talented songwriter as well as a musician. Someday, Elsie would write hillbilly tunes for him.

Jimmie's optimistic nature soon spurred him on to new show business enterprises. After scraping together some money, he invested in a traveling tent show that featured Hawaiian music. Since the performers carried their tent and bleachers with them, they never had to worry about finding a building in which to play. But they did sometimes have to worry about bad weather. One night, a bruising wind-and-rainstorm destroyed the show's tent and bleachers. With no place to perform, the actors and singers had to disband the show. Once again, Jimmie Rodgers was left jobless and broke.

Out of sheer desperation, Jimmie returned to railroad work for brief periods in 1925 and 1926. He knew that he was going against doctors' orders by going back to railroading. "But the doctors," he said to himself, "don't have to worry about feeding my family." Jimmie worked first as a brakeman for the Florida East Coast Railroad out of Miami, but soon the wet climate brought on a recurrence of his tuberculosis. Faced with bad health again, Jimmie decided to move his family to Tucson, Arizona, where he found work with the Southern Pacific line. The hot, dry air was better for him, but a brakeman's position was still too hard on Jimmie physically. He had to leave his job yet another time.

The Rodgers family decided to move again. They drove back to Meridian, where Carrie and their daughter stayed while Jimmie went on to Asheville, North Carolina. A friend had gotten him a job there as a city detective, and Jimmie obtained more work for himself as a building janitor and furnaceman. After a few months of quiet living in Asheville, Jimmie began to feel better. His health was improving steadily, and so was his financial situation. Carrie and their daughter soon joined Jimmie in Asheville, which eased the burden of loneliness for them all. They were a family once again.

Rodgers, nonetheless, felt frustrated. Music was in his blood. He had tasted just enough of the entertainment world to give him an appetite for more. And while he had not yet made any significant achievements in music, he still had confidence in himself. While analyzing his prospects for a career in music, Jimmie considered the state of the entertainment industry itself.

It was 1927, and the young radio industry was opening new doors for hillbilly performers all the time. Stations such as WSB in Atlanta, Georgia, WBAP in Fort Worth, Texas, WLS in Chicago, Illinois, and WSM in Nashville, Tennessee, were playing country music on many of their shows. And their audiences were growing. Some of the programs on these stations, such as the WLS "National Barn Dance" and the WSM "Barn Dance" (later to be renamed the "Grand Ole Opry"), were among the most popular in the country.

Because of radio, the country sound became very popular all across the nation by the late 1920s.

Individual performers and groups found radio invaluable because they always got more bookings for shows as a result of being on a broadcast. Such string bands as Dr. Humphrey Bate and his Possum Hunters and Gid Turner and the Skillet Lickers got their real starts on radio. And such artists as Fiddlin' John Carson and Uncle Dave Macon, known in the South for years, became famous throughout the United States because of radio.

If other folks could become famous over the radio, Jimmie thought, so could he. He told Carrie that he was going to try to get a few musicians together to form a band. They would play schoolhouses, taverns, and barn dances—wherever people

Jimmie Rodgers and the Entertainers

gathered to socialize, spend a few dollars, and listen to country music. Jimmie's idea was to get on the radio eventually and maybe even have his own show. His new band was to be called the "Jimmie Rodgers Entertainers."

In May 1927, the Entertainers got a job on WWNC Radio in Asheville. The local Chamber of Commerce hired Jimmie and his band to promote the city over radio. Although audience reaction to the band was good, the job didn't last long. Still, Jimmie did not get discouraged. At least he and the Entertainers could now bill themselves as radio stars.

After the radio job fell through, Jimmie and the band had a series of one-night stands throughout the Southeast. They soon found that life on the road was extremely uncertain. Sometimes the crowds were good, and the band was well paid for its trouble. But other times the band didn't even earn enough money to meet traveling expenses. Every place they appeared, though, they were received very warmly. People especially liked Jimmie's singing and yodeling. He was, without a doubt, the main attraction.

Jimmie soon began thinking about another avenue through which he might pursue a musical career—records. The record industry had begun more than 20 years before the radio industry. Unlike radio stations, record companies had not shown very much interest in hillbilly singers. Record company executives did not realize just how popular country music was until the beginning of radio, when the public started buying radio sets in order to hear country singers. When the record company executives saw their mistake, they sent out talent scouts to find and record hillbilly artists.

Carrie Rodgers knew how much Jimmie wanted to break into the recording industry, so she kept her ears open for any possibilities. One day, she heard about a talent scout who was planning to audition country performers in Bristol, Tennessee. The scout, whose name was Ralph Peer, worked for the Victor Talking Machine Company. Carrie suggested to her husband that he go to Bristol, and Jimmie agreed. He had already written to Victor, Brunswick, and other companies, asking for auditions, but his letter-writing campaign hadn't worked. Maybe the personal approach would.

Accompanied by his wife and daughter, Jimmie and his band headed for Bristol. They performed along the way to get money for gas and food. Jimmie, at this time, was still only one step ahead of poverty, but that would soon change. The meeting in Bristol between Rodgers and Peer would prove to be an important step in the development of both Jimmie Rodgers' career and the country music industry.

Jimmie Rodgers and Claude Grant, one of the Entertainers

The First Recording Session 5

R alph Peer was a pioneer in the country music industry. He worked behind the scenes, recording new singers and promoting them throughout the United States. Although the stars were the ones who got all the public attention, it was men like Ralph Peer who kept the recording industry going. Through their efforts, such talented people as Jimmie Rodgers were discovered and made stars.

By the time Peer came to Bristol, Tennessee, he had been in the record business for about 10 years. Much of his experience came not from staying in the big city but from traveling around the countryside. He would take his portable recording equipment from place to place, holding auditions. By traveling around so much, Peer was able to discover new markets as well as new talents. Knowing that blacks wanted to buy records made by black artists, he recorded singer Mamie Smith, thus opening another new market for the recording industry.

During his search for black talent in the rural South, Peer found that there was another untapped market for still another kind of music—hillbilly. Whites in the South were just as interested in hillbilly singing and playing as blacks were in blues music. Fiddlin' John Carson, a country musician who had gained popularity over Radio WSB in Atlanta, was recorded by Ralph Peer and Polk Brockman, an Okeh Record wholesale distributor. This recording marked the beginning of the commercial music industry; that is, Carson's release was the first country music record to be produced for nation-wide distribution.

The "new" sound—hillbilly—was strange to Peer's ears, and he really didn't think much of Carson's singing. Nonetheless, Fiddlin' John Carson's record sold so well that the Okeh Record Company sent him to New York to record more songs. Meanwhile, Peer was discovering other country talent, including Henry Whitter, Kelly Harrell, and Al Hopkins. Peer gave Hopkin's string band the name "The Hillbillies," which marked the first time that the word was used in an official way.

By 1927, Peer had left Okeh Records to run his own music publishing company. About that time, the Victor Talking Machine Company was looking for country artists of its own. Victor was the biggest company in the record industry, but it also was a conservative one. Its executives had been very cautious about getting into country music. But suddenly one of its singers of popular and light operatic music, Vernon Dalhart, became successful with country releases such as "The Wreck of the Old 97." This success convinced Victor executives that they should build up their country talent, so Ralph Peer was hired as a scout. The agreement was that Peer's publishing company would own the copyrights to songs recorded by Victor, and that he would receive royalties on record sales.

The word quickly spread whenever Peer was going to hold auditions in a particular town. Newspapers would carry stories announcing his schedule and plans, or else he would buy advertisements letting all the local talent know when he would be in town. When an interested person saw the news, he or she would tell another, who would in turn tell someone else. Sometimes so many musicians showed up to audition that there wasn't time to hear all of them. Of those who were auditioned, only a few ever became recording artists.

Ralph Peer, however, struck gold in Bristol that week in 1927. Within a few days, he had the good fortune to find not only Jimmie Rodgers but also another important talent. It was then that Peer recorded the Carter family—Sara, Maybelle, and A.P.—who one day would be known as the "First Family of Country Music." Peer at first was far more impressed with the Carters than with Rodgers. Because they had more musical experience than Rodgers, Peer had them make three records at Bristol. Jimmie made only one—and he almost lost the opportunity to do even that.

When Jimmie and the Entertainers got to Bristol, Jimmie was in for a shock. The rest of the Entertainers had decided to entertain without him. Jack Price, Jack Grant, and his brother Claude were going to make their own records under the name "Tenneva Ramblers." This name came from combining the names of Tennessee and Virginia, the

Ralph Peer and his wife remained close to Jimmie throughout his career. From left to right: *Jimmie Rodgers, Mrs. Peer, Anita Rodgers* (front), *Ralph Peer, and Carrie Rodgers*

two states in which Bristol was located. (One side of Main Street was in Tennessee and the other side in Virginia.)

There are conflicting stories on why Jimmie's group broke up. One possible reason was that the other members of the band may have been jealous of the attention Jimmie got as the main attraction. Another account was that Peer himself had suggested the split in the belief that Jimmie and the others were mismatched. But whatever the reason, Peer was not overly eager to audition Jimmie as a solo. Peer felt that the young man was relatively unknown, and without band support he probably wouldn't make much of an impact on the public.

For Jimmie Rodgers, this audition was the crucial point in his career, and he knew it. He not only had lost his band, but he also was having coughing spells. A less determined person would have gone home in discouragement, but Jimmie wasn't ready to give up. Besides, there was no job for him to go home to. He could no longer work for the railroad. And if he couldn't be a singer, what would happen to him and his family? Jimmie had no choice but to stay in Bristol and persuade Peer to let him sing.

On August 4, 1927, Jimmie, accompanied by his wife and daughter, climbed the stairs to the third floor of the building in Bristol that housed Peer's temporary recording studio. Jimmie, wearing a faded old suit, curled his hands tensely around his

ancient Martin guitar while the microphone and
other equipment were being set up. He was going
to sing two selections, both of which surprised his
wife when she found out what they were.

Carrie had thought that one of Jimmie's songs
would be his own "T for Texas." This tune had
been well received at performances in and around
Asheville. It included falsetto, or high-pitched
singing, plus some unique yodeling that he had
begun polishing a few years earlier.

But Jimmie knew instinctively that he should
not sing that song at his first recording session.
"T for Texas" was a fast novelty tune in which he
sang about "the gal who made a wreck out of me."
He was afraid that the Victor executives in New
York would be so caught up in the lyrics that they
wouldn't pay enough attention to his voice. Instead
Jimmie selected two slower songs for his test record.
One was a standard mountain lullaby, "Sleep, Baby,
Sleep." The other was "Soldier's Sweetheart," which
Jimmie had written about a railroad friend who
had been killed in France in World War I.

Jimmie had definite ideas about how a song
should be sung at an audition or at a performance.
He enunciated plainly so that listeners could
understand him. His biggest complaint about
other vocalists, was, "Can't make out a word they're
sayin'." And he felt that musical accompaniment
should enhance the voice, not drown it out.

In spite of Jimmie's high set of musical standards, Ralph Peer was unawed by Jimmie's performance that day. If Peer had really liked the performance, Jimmie would have cut more than one record. Yet Peer was not blind to Jimmie's talent. He detected an appealing quality of warmth and feeling in Jimmie's style, and may have had a hunch about the commercial possibilities of Jimmie's singing. That day he signed Rodgers to a contract, and then did something he was not obliged to do. He reached into his pocket, dug out a 20-dollar bill, and handed it to Jimmie.

The Rodgers were grateful. Quickly they moved from their cheap room in Bristol into a better hotel. Jimmie wanted to feel like somebody important, if only for that night.

Jimmie dressed as a cowboy for a publicity photo

Blue Yodeler's Paradise

6

Ralph Peer sent Jimmie's test record to New York. There, Victor executives listened to it and were impressed enough to produce and distribute it. A few months later, Jimmie received his first royalty check, for $27.43. It was not exactly a kingly sum, and the amount indicated that the record was not selling very well. The check, however, was only a shadow of what was to come. It marked the beginning of the end of poverty and hardship for Jimmie. He was about to begin a real singing career and was well on his way to becoming a star.

While waiting for the sales of his first record to pick up, Jimmie moved his family to Washington, D.C., where he found singing jobs in nightclubs and movie theaters. He had trouble holding any one job for long, though, because of his illness. Periodically he would have to quit work and stay in bed to recover from terrible coughing spells and fever. Carrie kept the family going by working as a waitress.

After a few months in Washington, Jimmie began to grow impatient with the Victor Recording Company. He still had not heard from Peer or from the Victor executives, so he went to New York. With characteristic determination and confidence, Jimmie telephoned Peer. "I just happened to be in town," he said, "and decided to see if you need any more recordings."

At that point, Jimmie's first record was still selling slowly. But Peer must have been following his original hunch about Jimmie's potential, for he set up a second recording session in November 1927. It was to be held at the Victor studio, an old converted Baptist church in Camden, New Jersey.

Jimmie, no doubt, did a lot of thinking about his choice of material before arriving at the studio. For his first session, Jimmie had chosen slow-paced numbers, because he had wanted the record company executives to be impressed with his voice rather than with his songs. But now it was time for Jimmie to use his very best songs.

Rodgers cut four titles at his second session. Among them was "T for Texas," later renamed "Blue Yodel No. 1" because it was the first in a series of 12 blue yodel numbers that Rodgers would record. There is no way of knowing, of course, what would have happened if Rodgers had recorded "T for Texas" at his first session. Perhaps in holding back this song, he had been overly cautious. Perhaps he would have become a star much sooner had he recorded it. Then again, maybe his timing was exactly right. In any event, there is little doubt that Jimmie's first blue yodel tune was a hit.

Within about three months, the record was among the best sellers in the country. Peer then knew that he had been right about Jimmie, but one thing bothered him. He felt that Jimmie did not sing enough of his own material. Peer advised him to work on new songs, like blue yodels, that would reflect his feeling and background. "You'll sell more records than if you recorded songs by New York writers," said Peer.

Jimmie agreed. In an instant, he was on the telephone to his sister-in-law, Elsie McWilliams, whose songwriting ability he remembered from their days together in the dance combo. At Jimmie's request, she came to Washington to work with him. She later went on tours with him, writing songs and rewriting old material. She often composed and rewrote hurriedly in hotel rooms or in recording studios so that Jimmie would have the latest material possible. Altogether, Elsie worked with her brother-in-law on about 38 songs, although her name wasn't on everything she wrote or co-wrote. Among the many songs that she worked on were "Sailor's Plea," "I'm Lonely and Blue," "Mississippi Moon," and "My Little Lady."

By early 1928, Rodgers' record company was billing Jimmie as an "Exclusive Victor Recording Star." His nicknames, the Singing Brakeman and America's Blue Yodeler, were also beginning to capture the imagination of the country music public. By February 1928, Jimmie was so successful that Ralph Peer arranged a third recording session for him. This session was only one in a long series of recording sessions that would take place in the next few years.

Six months after Jimmie had received his first royalty check for $27.43, he was earning about $2,000 a month in royalties. It was like paradise for someone who had struggled for so long. Jimmie was an overnight success to some, but the seemingly quick rise to fame had taken a painfully long time as far as he was concerned.

The Rodgers' recordings that caught the public's fancy represented a remarkable variety of themes. Jimmie wrote and sang about jail, gamblers, good marriages, bad marriages, babies, love, and death. There were sentimental songs such as "Daddy and Home" (one of Rodgers' favorites) and "I'm Lonely and Blue," railroad songs such as "Train Whistle Blues" and "Mystery of Number Five," cowboy songs such as "Yodeling Cowboy" and "Yodeling Ranger," blues pieces such as "Brakeman's Blues" and "Never No Mo' Blues," hobo songs such as "Hobo Bill's Last Ride" and "Hobo's Meditation,"

and slightly naughty songs such as "Frankie and
Johnny" and "Pistol Packin' Papa." At least two of
Jimmie's songs, "TB Blues" and "Whippin' That
Old TB," were about his own disease.

The background sounds on Jimmie's records
were as varied as the subjects for his songs. Besides
yodeling and guitar picking, he accompanied himself on his train songs with whistling. He became
very good at imitating the sound of a locomotive
whistle. Quite different from his train songs were
his songs with Hawaiian musical backing. Other
songs had elements of pop music or jazz. On his
"Blue Yodel No. 9," Jimmie was backed by jazz
musicians Louis Armstrong and Earl "Fatha"
Hines. Completely unprejudiced, Jimmie often
recorded with a group composed partly or entirely
of blacks. There is nothing unusual about this
today, but it certainly wasn't usual back in the late
1920s and early 30s.

Jimmie's ability to do many different kinds of
songs was admired by other performers, among
them Jimmie's friend Gene Austin. Gene was a
popular singer known for the song "My Blue
Heaven." He admired Jimmie's versatility and felt
that he would do well playing in person in a large
theater. Austin got Jimmie a guest spot at the Earle
Theater in Washington, D.C., where Jimmie sang
"Frankie and Johnny." That song proved Austin
right. Jimmie got 16 encores and finally had to

leave the stage because of exhaustion.

From Austin came the inspiration for another idea. This idea came at a time when Jimmie was earning the most money of his life, about $100,000 a year. The two men and their families had gone sailing together on Austin's yacht, appropriately named the "Blue Heaven." Shortly thereafter, Jimmie began building a mansion in Kerrville, Texas, a town he selected because it was near a tuberculosis sanitorium. Even as Austin had symbolically named his yacht, so Jimmie named his new home. He called the mansion "Blue Yodeler's Paradise." It was his pride and joy, a symbol of his accomplishments and an indication that he—for what would be a very short time—was on top of the entertainment world.

A prosperous Jimmie Rodgers in Kerrville,
Texas, where he made his home in later years

The Last Recording Session 7

Success did not change Jimmie Rodgers. He was the same likeable, fun-loving fellow that he had been when he was poor. But now, instead of slipping 50 cents into a hobo's hand, Jimmie was handing out 50-dollar bills without blinking an eye.

Jimmie knew that he was a soft touch for a hard-luck story. Not only did he give to the poor, but he also spent money as fast as he earned it—much to the dismay of his wife. He felt that money was made to be spent, and this is the philosophy on which he based his living habits. Jimmie's luxurious mansion, his expensive automobiles equipped with the latest gadgets, his custom-tailored suits, and his $1,500 guitars were more than status symbols to him. They represented everything that he had missed in his youth. It was as if Jimmie were trying to make up for lost time.

In spite of all the securities and comforts of home, Jimmie felt restless. He was always on the move, looking for something else to do, somewhere else to play. Part of this restlessness was due to his constant need for cash, but part was probably due to his childhood. He had worked hard ever since he was a boy. Because of this, Jimmie's career was packed with one recording session after another. He averaged about 20 releases a year from 1928 to 1932. He also made hundreds of personal appearances in that time, but traveling was becoming ever more difficult and tiring for him.

When Jimmie went on a long tour, he tried to get several things done at once. In the fall of 1929, while in Camden to record, Jimmie made his only film. It was just 10 minutes long. "Short subjects," as such films were called, were common in that day. They were used by movie houses to supplement full-length films. Jimmie's movie, *The Singing Brakeman,* was a hit, although it had no significant story line. It was simply a showcase for three of Jimmie's songs, "Waiting for the Train," "Dear Old Dad," and "T for Texas," which the audience loved.

In the early 1930s, Jimmie began playing theaters in the vaudeville circuit. A vaudeville show was much like today's television variety show, except that its performers traveled from one theater to another to do their acts. Jimmie soon became a leading attraction in these shows and played in many vaudeville theaters in the South. He had plans to tour nationally, but he was never well enough to do so. In addition to his theater performances, Jimmie was much in demand at various civic events, especially in Texas, his adopted home state. He also made many benefit appearances.

In 1931 Jimmie and Will Rogers, the famous humorist, participated in a series of benefits for victims of floods, drought, and the unemployment caused by the Depression. The two men became close friends. Will Rogers, whose name was spelled without a *d*, called Jimmie Rodgers, with a *d*, "my distant son." He wryly referred to the singer's "Blue Yodeler's Paradise" as "the home you built with your throat."

For personal appearances, Jimmie usually wore a white or tan lightweight suit, a polka dot tie, and

Jimmie in his short film, The Singing Brakeman

a straw hat. Occasionally he wore a railroad brakeman's uniform or cowboy clothes. These outfits,
however, were primarily for publicity and picture-
taking.

Jimmie's performances, like his slouchy straw
hats, were characterized by an easy informality and
warmth. During a show, he was fond of propping
his foot up on a chair and cradling his guitar across
his knee. Then he would shut his eyes and pour
out his soul into the microphone. Often Jimmie
would mutter aloud such phrases as "Hey, hey,
hey" and "Play that thing, boy." He joked with the
audience, too, which added to the informality of
the performance. Jimmie's act was relatively short
by modern standards. It lasted only about 20 minutes, which was all he was able to stand physically.
Even then, he was often in pain while performing.

By 1932, Jimmie's health was failing with alarm-
ing rapidity. He had to remain at home for longer
and longer periods before he could muster the
strength to go on tour again. Medical expenses
continued to rise. The cost of maintaining a mansion was, of course, substantial, and Jimmie simply
had not saved enough money to live in such splen-
dor. He was finally forced to sell "Blue Yodeler's
Paradise" and move his family to a modest home
in San Antonio.

There, Jimmie got a twice-weekly radio program
on Station KMAC. The program unfortunately

came to a halt in January 1933, when Jimmie once again had to go into the hospital. He came home a month later, and was confined to bed for more than two months. Time was clearly running out for Jimmie Rodgers. He and the doctors knew that he probably did not have long to live. In fact, the doctors could not understand how Jimmie had managed to sing at all. His only chance to survive even a few years, everyone agreed, was to rest.

But Jimmie decided to have one more recording session. The royalties from his new releases, he reasoned, would provide some security for Carrie and Anita. Jimmie went to New York and began the session on May 17, 1933. Twenty-four songs were to be recorded, but the process was agonizingly slow. At the conclusion of each number, Rodgers had to lie down on a cot brought into the studio especially for him. A private nurse gave him medicine to ease his tortured, diseased lungs and body-shaking cough.

By May 24, only 12 of the 24 songs had been recorded, and Jimmie was too weak to do any more. Among the songs he did complete were "I'm Free from the Chain Gang Now" and "Yodeling My Way Back Home." Jimmie wheezed out his last note and then had to be taken back to the hotel. The next day he started hemorrhaging, and slipped into a coma. In the early morning hours of May 26, 1933, Jimmie Rodgers, aged 35, died in his hotel room.

*This monument honoring Jimmie Rodgers
was erected in Meridian, Mississippi, in 1953.*

Home to Meridian 8

Jimmie Rodgers' body was brought back to Meridian, Mississippi, to be buried beside that of his daughter, June Rebecca. The mournful nostalgia of this last train ride was much like Jimmie's railroad songs, in which he sang about "Ben Dewberry's final run" or "Hobo Bill's last ride." As Jimmie's funeral train crept into Meridian, engineer Homer Jenkins pulled the whistle cord in one long, sorrowful blast. It was truly a railroad man's tribute.

Relatives and friends were gathered in the terminal when the train arrived. Many were crying. Jimmie had been *their* boy, and his songs had expressed their feelings, hopes, and fears. He had spoken for all of them as well as for himself.

The loss was deeply felt in other parts of the country, too, particularly among young performers who idolized Jimmie. One of them, Ernest Tubb, met Jimmie's widow years later. Carrie was so touched by Tubb's devotion to her husband that she gave him one of Jimmie's guitars. She also

managed to help him in his career. Tubb ulti-
mately became a country star himself, as did Hank
Snow, another performer who admired Jimmie.
Hank even named his son after Jimmie. (The
Reverend Jimmie Rodgers Snow is now a minister
in Nashville.)

Tubb and Snow were among those instrumental
in planning a "Jimmie Rodgers Day," held May 26,
1953, on the 20th anniversary of Rodgers' death.
Nearly 30,000 people attended ceremonies in Meridian that day. During the ceremonies, a stone

*Ernest Tubb with Carrie Rodgers on "Jimmie
Rodgers Day." Tubb was a devoted admirer of Jimmie.*

monument purchased by the two stars was unveiled, and an old steam locomotive donated by railroad men was dedicated as a memorial. There were speeches by political dignitaries and by leaders from the entertainment world as well. In the evening, a free show was put on by Red Foley and the Carter Family. The one-day event subsequently led to the formation of the Jimmie Rodgers Memorial Festival, Inc., a nonprofit organization that holds week-long observances annually in Meridian.

Rodgers' contributions were recognized in yet another city. Nashville, Tennessee, the capital of country music, also claimed Jimmie because he had been such a pioneer. He was country music's first singing star, and by the 1950s many others had followed in his footsteps: Roy Acuff, Hank Williams, Eddy Arnold, Red Foley, Ernest Tubb, and Hank Snow, to mention only a few. Thanks to Jimmie, country music had finally achieved the national attention it deserved.

The Country Music Association was founded in the 1950s to promote the welfare of the industry, to preserve its tradition, and to plan for the future. In 1961, the association established the Country Music Hall of Fame to recognize and honor those individuals most responsible for the development and continuing growth of the industry. The first person elected was Jimmie Rodgers, the Father of Country Music.

Jimmie's plaque is in the Hall of Fame Museum in Nashville, where it has been viewed and read by hundreds of thousands of people. The thoughtful message inscribed on it speaks for everyone who admires the music that grew up with the country:

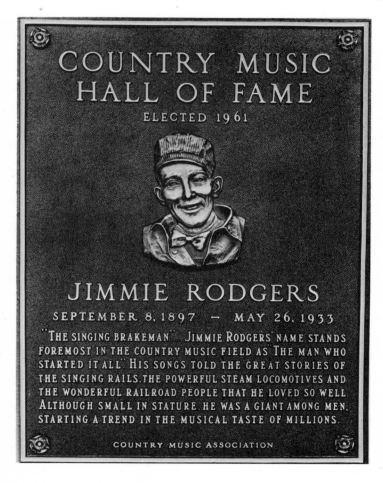

COUNTRY MUSIC HALL OF FAME
ELECTED 1961

JIMMIE RODGERS
SEPTEMBER 8, 1897 — MAY 26, 1933
"THE SINGING BRAKEMAN." JIMMIE RODGERS' NAME STANDS FOREMOST IN THE COUNTRY MUSIC FIELD AS "THE MAN WHO STARTED IT ALL." HIS SONGS TOLD THE GREAT STORIES OF THE SINGING RAILS, THE POWERFUL STEAM LOCOMOTIVES AND THE WONDERFUL RAILROAD PEOPLE THAT HE LOVED SO WELL. ALTHOUGH SMALL IN STATURE, HE WAS A GIANT AMONG MEN, STARTING A TREND IN THE MUSICAL TASTE OF MILLIONS.

COUNTRY MUSIC ASSOCIATION

Recordings of Jimmie Rodgers

This list is limited only to those Jimmie Rodgers' recordings that are currently available. The albums include a wide selection of the artist's most representative work.

RECORD	LABEL	RECORD NO.
All about Trains	*Victor*	*ANL 1-1052*
The Best of the Legendary Jimmie Rodgers	*Victor*	*LSP 3315*
Country Music	*New World*	*287*
Country Music Hall of Fame	*Victor*	*LPM 2531*
Jimmie the Kid	*Victor*	*LPM 2213*
My Rough and Rowdy Ways	*Victor*	*ANL 1-1209*
My Time Ain't Long	*Victor*	*LPM 2865*
Never No Mo' Blues	*Victor*	*LPM 1232*
The Short But Brilliant Life of Jimmie Rodgers	*Victor*	*LPM 2634*
This Is Jimmie Rodgers	*Victor*	*VPS 6091*
Train Whistle Blues	*Victor*	*LPM 1640*

Index